William Shakespeare's

Macbeth

TEACHER'S RESOURCE BOOK

Philip Page and Marilyn Pettit

ILLUSTRATED BY
Philip Page

Published in association with

Hodder & Stoughton
A MEMBER OF THE HODDER HEADLINE GROUP

Acknowledgments
The publisher would like to thank the following copyright holders for permission to reproduce their photographs:
Pages 8, 12, 17, 45 © Donald Cooper, Photostage
Page 4 Phil Page
Pages 36, 39 Shakespeare Centre Library, Stratford-Upon-Avon

Every effort has been made to trace copyright holders of material reproduced in this book. Any rights not acknowledged here will be acknowledged in subsequent printings if notice is given to the publisher.

Orders: please contact Bookpoint Ltd, 130 Milton Park, Abingdon, Oxon OX14 4SB, Telephone: (44) 01235 827720, Fax: (44) 01235 400454. Lines are open from 9.00–6.00, Monday to Saturday, with a 24 hour message answering service. You can also order through our website www.hodderheadline.co.uk

British Library Cataloguing in Publication Data
A catalogue record for this title is available from The British Library

ISBN 0 340 74299 2

First published 1999
Impression number   10 9 8
Year   2005 2004

Papers used in this book are natural, renewable and recyclable products. They are made from wood grown in sustainable forests. The logging and manufacturing processes conform to the environmental regulations of the country of origin.

Cover illustration by Lee Stinton
Typeset by Fakenham Photosetting Ltd, Fakenham, Norfolk
Printed in Great Britain for Hodder & Stoughton Educational, a division of Hodder Headline, 338 Euston Road, London NW1 3BH by Hobbs the Printers, Totton, Hampshire.

Contents

Introduction

The worksheets in this Teacher's Resource Book are intended to be used with *Livewire Shakespeare: Macbeth*. All references, such as page numbers, relate to that book.

The worksheets address the pupils directly, so that, where appropriate, there is opportunity for pupil autonomy. However, the majority of the tasks lend themselves to teacher/pupil/class interaction.

They attempt to provide a background to Shakespeare and his theatre, so that the play can be viewed as a *stage play*, rather than a text. This approach is continued throughout the book.

All four language modes: Speaking, Listening, Reading and Writing are considered in the tasks.

There are a variety of activities, so that pupils experience: collaborative and individual work; a wide range of written pieces; drama pieces; and debate and discussion with reference to both Shakespearean language and today's English.

The activities have been devised with the SATs and the 'teenage classroom' in mind.

Together with the development of an understanding of Shakespeare, the emphasis is on fun, where pupils learn to support and evaluate their work.

Who was Shakespeare? I

Lots of people think that Shakespeare is one of the greatest writers who has ever lived. That's why we study his plays today. That's why pupils from other countries study his plays too!

Not much is known about his life, though. Some of the known facts can be found in the letter on Sheet 2. The letter has been written by one pupil to another.

1 Some of the words in the letter have been jumbled up. Rearrange the letters so that the words make sense. If you need help, use the words in the box below to help you.

Words to help

```
school   Shakespeare   married   exciting   children
London   Stratford   finish   three   father   acted
poems   gravestone
```

2 What have you learnt about Shakespeare today?
Write a FACT SHEET about Shakespeare that might go into a book for young children. You could draw your own cartoon character to give the facts.

For example:

(Continued on Sheet 2)

I

Who was Shakespeare? 2

(Continued from Sheet 1)

Dear Sandip,

We had a lesson on Shakespeare today. Hey, we learnt a lot. Bet you don't know some of this!

We think that **Sseeehparka** was born in Stratford-upon-Avon in 1564. Most people think that he went to **hsoolc** in Stratford. Lots of people think that he didn't **shifni** school, but that he had to leave to help his **threfa** with his business.

He got **mrrdiea** in 1582 when he was 18! He and his wife, Anne Hathaway, had **eethr** children: Susanna, Hamnet, and Judith! Guest what – Hamnet died! Susanna had a daughter who had no **cirlhden** and Judith's children all died! That's sad! He had no descendants!

Did you know that some people say that he had to leave **traStofdr** because he stole a deer? Anyway, he went to **Lndoon** and wrote plays and **ctdea** in some. He wrote **oepms** too!

He died in 1616! He's buried in Stratford and, think about this … there are some words on his **vegrsotnea** that put a curse on anyone who dares to move his bones!!

I bet he had an **xctignei** life.

Well, I'll sign off now,

Christine

I've got a bone to pick with you!

Shakespeare would certainly have **'a bone to pick'** with you, if you moved his bones!

That's a strange phrase. Has anybody ever said that to you? Was it when they wanted to complain about something you had done? Was it when somebody was angry with you over something?

1 Shakespeare is buried in Stratford-upon-Avon and there is a curse written on his gravestone. Read the curse below and try to put it into Modern English. Remember that they didn't spell like we do!

GOOD FREND FOR IESVS SAKE FORBEARE,
TO DIGG ϷE DVST ENCLOASED HEARE.
BLESE BE Ẏ MAN Ẏ SPARES ϷES STONES,
AND CVRST BE HE Ẏ MOVES MY BONES.

The gravestone says, **'cursed be he who moves my bones'**. There was a charnel-house near the church in Stratford. A charnel-house is a building where dead bodies and bones are kept. In Shakespeare's time, if a new grave was needed, old bones would be dug up and stored in this building.

Shakespeare couldn't have been very happy about this. No wonder he put a curse on anyone who dug him up! No wonder he would have had a **'bone to pick'** with anyone who disturbed him!
It worked too – his body is still there!

2 Write another curse that would scare people so much that they would leave his resting place in peace.

When you have finished, share your curse with the class and see if you came up with the same frightening ideas. You might like to display them all.

Behind the scenes at the Globe Theatre I

1 Read the interview on Sheet 2, between a reporter and a man who acted in Shakespeare's plays at the Globe. The interview is made up, but it is based on facts.

Using the information in it, you're going to write a speech that a **guide** might give to **tourists** who come to visit the Globe Theatre in London in our times.
Remember that a **guide** has to interest people and tell them lots of facts about the theatre.

2 Plan your speech first, using the actor's answers to help you. You can also go into the Globe Theatre Website on the Internet (http://shakespeares-globe.org). That will give you some more ideas. Ask your teacher to help you with this.

3 After you have written out the speech, practise how you will say it. When you're ready, you can perform it in front of your class or a small group. They can take the part of the **tourists**.
You might begin like this:

Good afternoon. Welcome to the Globe Theatre. Today I will be your guide ...

(Continued on Sheet 2)

Behind the scenes at the Globe Theatre 2

(Continued from Sheet 1)

Reporter: Do you enjoy acting?

Actor: Oh yes, it's fun. As you can see, the stage has three sides and the audience can stand around those sides. They are very close indeed. Sometimes, they even call out to us on stage – it makes acting very exciting and different every time. They can be so noisy!

Reporter: When do most plays take place?

Actor: In the afternoon, when it's good weather. It's hopeless when it's raining. No-one wants to stand and watch us then! And of course, we have to perform the play when there is enough daylight.

Reporter: So, how do people know when a play is about to start?

Actor: A flag goes up and a trumpet plays, then people come along. They pay a penny to stand; another penny to sit in the seats around the standing area. It's warmer under the thatched roof.

Reporter: You don't have many props do you?

Actor: No, that's right. We have boards sometimes to tell the audience what town we're supposed to be in. We have a backcloth which tells them if it's a comedy or tragedy! And really, we have to use our lines to say what time of day it is, and where we are.

Reporter: Can you explain that?

Actor: Well, if we're in a forest, our lines will mention a forest. If it's night time, our lines will have something about the moon or how dark it is. We do have lovely costumes though. Some of them are VERY expensive!

Reporter: Do you have any sound effects?

Actor: Not many. Sometimes, we have a trumpet or a cannon firing, but that can be dangerous. One time, the theatre burnt down after a cannon was fired. It caught the straw roof and that was the end of a lovely theatre!

Reporter: I can't see any curtains.

Actor: Curtains? No we don't have them – we show that a scene has changed by using two lines that rhyme! Of course, we can't have everybody dead on stage either. Without curtains, they'd have to get up and walk off and everybody would laugh! So we always have somebody to carry them off.

Reporter: Thank you very much for your time.

Actor: A pleasure!

Under cover of darkness

Let's put those words into some sentences:

What Leon was doing had to be kept a secret, so he did it **under cover of darkness**.
Ranjit felt really guilty about doing this and that's why she did it **under cover of darkness**.

1 What do you think those words **'under cover of darkness'** mean?
2 What might you want to keep secret? What might you feel guilty about?

Look at the cover of *Macbeth*. It is certainly in darkness. This might suggest that the play is about secrets and guilt. **Symbols** can also suggest things to you; they give you ideas. This time look at the **symbols** on the cover: **a candle, a crown, a dagger dripping blood**!

3 Decide what the story might be about just by thinking of these **symbols**. To help you, answer these questions:

● Who wears a crown? Whose blood might be on the dagger?
● Why would someone want to use a candle in the middle of the night?

Look further into the picture.

● What kind of building can you see?
● Does it look a welcoming place?
● Can you see shadows on the wall?
● What might they be watching out for?
● One person looks smaller than the other. What might that tell you?

Share your ideas with the class.
Now read on and see if you were close to the truth!

Which costume for which witch? 1

The first **things** to come onto stage in this play are the WITCHES! They come on to the sound of thunder and lightning. Today's theatres can be made to go very dark, but on Shakespeare's stage, the audience would have to imagine the storm.

1 With a partner, think of how you want the audience to feel in this opening scene.
Look at the adjectives below. Decide which adjectives best suit the mood you want the audience to feel.

scared   worried   happy   sad   anxious   uneasy cheerful

2 Now think about the costumes the Witches will wear. In the pictures in your book, the Witches are all dressed in similar robes. Do you want all your witches to look the same?

- Have you noticed that **one** witch seems to know more than the others?
- Look at the witch on the **right** side of the second picture.
  - Follow what **it** says through the two pages.
  - **It** knows when the battle will finish – can you find that line?
  - **It** knows who they will meet – can you find that line?
  - **It** tells the cat and toad that they are coming – can you find the word?
  - Perhaps this witch is different?
- Have you noticed that the first witch to speak asks the questions? – Perhaps this one isn't so powerful?

What colours do you want your witches in? Frightening and violent ones?

(Continued on Sheet 2)

Which costume for which witch? 2

(Continued from Sheet 1)

3 Look at the picture of the Witches from a play performed at Stratford. The Witches here have beards.

How will your witches have their hair? Long? Short? Should they be bald?

Will you make sure they are female/male/or neither?

You must decide and **draw** your choices. You must be able to **explain** your choices to the rest of the class.

Staging a scene

Read Act 1: Scene 3 on pages 5 and 6 again.
You are going to **dramatise** this scene and present it to the rest of your class.
You will need a group of FIVE.

1 Decide what parts you will play. Decide whether you are going to use Shakespeare's language or **translate** it into Modern English. You will need to **read** your parts together, before you get up from your seats and add actions to your words, so that you get your voices right.

2 Think about:

- Will any of you raise your voices or shout?
- What will the Witches' voices sound like?
- Will any of you sound bossy at some stage?
- Will you sound puzzled and confused some times?

3 Once you are happy with your voices, decide on the actions you want. Remember, the clues are in the words. There are some ideas below to help you:

- Will Banquo turn his body towards the Witches on the words, '**Live you?**'
- What will the Witches do when they are greeting Macbeth. Will they bow, raise their arms, what else?
- What has Macbeth done to make Banquo say, '**why do you start and seem to fear?**'
- What is Macbeth doing when Banquo says, '**he seems rapt withal**'?
- What will the Witches be doing when they speak to Banquo? Will they circle him? Will they point at him?
- How do they vanish? What will Banquo and Macbeth do when they disappear?
- How will those two notice that someone is coming?

4 When you have matched your words with the actions, practise, and show it to your class.

On the one hand ... but on the other ...

These words are used to show that there is more than one way of looking at things. If you read pages 7 and 8 again, you will see that Banquo and Macbeth are thinking about the Witches and their predictions, but they have very different ideas.

1 Decide what their thoughts are by reading the lines below.

What? Can the Devil speak true?

'Tis strange: and oftentimes to win us to our harm, the instruments of Darkness tell us truths; win us with honest trifles, to betray's.

Glamis and Thane of Cawdor: the greatest is behind.

This supernatural soliciting cannot be ill; cannot be good. If ill, why hath it given me earnest of success commencing in a truth?

If good, why do I yield to that suggestion whose horrid image doth unfix my hair and make my seated heart knock at my ribs ...?

2 Now you are ready to write up your piece.

On the one hand, Banquo thinks ...   but on the other, Macbeth thinks ...

'To my dear wife': writing a letter

Look at page 10 again.
Lady Macbeth has just read a letter from Macbeth. She must be holding it in her hand as she stands on stage.

Below is the letter that Macbeth might have written to his wife. Fill in the blanks so that the letter makes sense.

To my dear _____,

We won the _____ against the enemy of Scotland.

I have some exciting _____ to tell you.

When Banquo and I were returning from the battle, we met _____ very strange women on the heath. They seemed to be _____, but they had beards! You'll never _____ what they said – that I would be Thane of Cawdor! If that wasn't enough, they also said I will be _____.

And then two men arrived to tell me that Duncan was making me Thane of _____!

Can you believe that? Who was the Thane of Cawdor has been _____. He was a traitor!

Well, if I am to be king, just think what that will make you – my _____!

I love you so much that I really wanted to _____ this with you.

I'll be with you soon. I have sent this ahead, so that you know _____ that has happened.

Your faithful husband, Macbeth

Words to help you

queen   everything   wife   king   three   Cawdor
guess   women   share   news   executed

A really nasty piece of work! I

A really nasty piece of work – that is what lots of people say about Lady Macbeth.

1 What proof have we got to say that she is evil and cruel?

Look at page 10. She has read Macbeth's letter and now she is talking to herself. She thinks that her husband is kind. She thinks that he is ambitious, but not mean enough to do anything to become king.

2 From what you know of Macbeth, would you say that he is kind?

(Continued on Sheet 2)

A really nasty piece of work! 2

(Continued from Sheet 1)

3 Read the lines that follow. They are in Modern English. Match them up with Shakespeare's lines.

- Come here quickly, so that I can talk you into doing something to become king!
- I call on the Spirits to make me cruel.
- I call upon the night. I want it to be as dark as Hell, so that nobody can see what I am going to do.

You have just found the proof of Lady Macbeth's **cruelty** and her **evil**.

You can find more proof, by reading what she tells Macbeth to do.

4 Again, read the Modern English and match it up with Shakespeare's lines.

- You've got to fool everyone ... so act as everyone will expect you to act.
- You've got to welcome him, and be nice to him.
- You've got to look as if you are really innocent, but under it all, you've got to be thinking mean thoughts!
- We've got to sort this Duncan out.
- Just leave this to me OK?

5 Now that you have read her lines again, do you agree that she is a **nasty piece of work**? Can you find anything about her to like?

She *does* love Macbeth after all. She *only* wants the best for him. She'll help him become king. She's a clever woman!

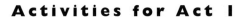

Having second thoughts

What has happened to Macbeth so far?

- The Witches told him he would be Thane of Cawdor ... and he was!
- They told him he would be king!
- His wife told him he would be king!
- His wife told him that she would sort out a plan to make sure that he became king!

Now Macbeth is having second thoughts. He doesn't know what to do.

Read page 13 again. Think about his arguments for and against killing Duncan.

- If it was done fast, and I could be sure of being king, I'd go ahead and do it.
- Wait! I might be judged here!
- He trusts me – I'm one of his men. I should be protecting him, not killing him.
- He's in my castle as well! And he's such a good person.
- All I have to make me kill him, is ambition – nothing else!

1 Imagine you're his good friend. Using four boxes, draw a comic strip of yourself giving Macbeth advice

2 In another comic strip, you could be one of the Witches. You want to get him into trouble. This time draw yourself as a Witch, giving him advice!

3 Make a group of three and act out your comic strips. Now you have the idea of Macbeth's **conscience** – his thoughts pulling him two ways. Whoever is playing Macbeth must use their voice, face and body to show Macbeth's feelings. Show your piece to the class.

The argument between husband and wife

You have already seen that Macbeth has had **second thoughts**.

When he talks to his wife again, he tells her that he will not go ahead and kill Duncan.

1 The following sentences are written in Modern English. They are mixed up. What you have to do is work out what he says and what she replies to make him agree to carry out the murder. Use pages 14–15 to help you.

- Be brave and we won't fail.
- He's been good to me lately and rewarded me.
- So, what made you break your promise to me?
- What if we fail?
- Would you really be a coward?
- Lots of people think so much of me now!
- I'd kill my own baby, if I had to, if I had promised you such a thing!
- Were you just messing about before when you said you wanted to be king?
- You wanted to do it, but you didn't have the chance ... now you've got the chance!
- I'll do anything any other man will do.

2 Now write down what Lady Macbeth's murder plan is! To help you, answer these questions:

- Will Duncan be awake or asleep?
- What will happen to his guards after they have drunk, but before Duncan is killed?
- What will they do to the guards after Duncan is dead?
- How will Lady Macbeth and Macbeth act when the King is found dead?

3 In pairs, use the information you have just collected and dramatise the scene between Lady Macbeth and her husband.

My mind's made up!

Macbeth has been thinking hard about what he has to do. He's had **second thoughts**. By the end of Act 1, he has agreed to kill Duncan.

1 Imagine that you are **Macbeth**. Just before you go to kill Duncan, you have a chance to write your diary entry for the day.
What a lot has happened. Write down as much as you can, explaining all that has taken place and how you are feeling now.

You might include:

- the battle
- the Witches and their predictions coming true
- Duncan rewarding you
- your wife and her suggestions of murder
- your worries at first about your future
- your wife's plan and how it made you feel that anything is possible!

2 Now imagine that you are **Lady Macbeth**. Just before you help with the plan to kill Duncan, imagine that you are in your room, brushing your hair, in front of a mirror. You talk to yourself. This is called a **monologue**. In your monologue, you might include:

- your worries about Macbeth because he was fighting a battle
- your relief when you got the letter – he was alive!
- your excitement when you read it and realised what it meant
- how you managed to think evil thoughts even when you were welcoming Duncan
- the problems you had making your husband see that the plan to kill the King would work
- your worries about Macbeth, now that he is about to do the deed!

Who's sorry now? 1

Read pages 18 and 19 again. Macbeth has murdered Duncan. He is already sorry that he has done such an awful thing.

1 The script on Sheet 2 retells that scene in Modern English. Lady Macbeth's words have been done for you.
Put Macbeth's words into Modern English so that when you and a partner read the scene, it will make sense.

2 When you have written Macbeth's words, you are ready to read it with a partner.
Practise until you are happy with your reading. Remember that you must think about:

- what your voices will sound like – whispers?
- how you will be moving, and what you will be looking at – over your shoulder? at your hands? at the door?
- what Lady Macbeth does when she sees the daggers.
- how you might jump when you get scared.

3 You can now act it out in front of the class.
Listen to what your class says about your piece. This will help you to improve your work.

(Continued on Sheet 2)

Who's sorry now? 2

(Continued from Sheet 1)

Lady Macbeth: I put the daggers ready. He couldn't miss them. I'd have killed Duncan if he hadn't looked a bit like my father.

Macbeth:

Lady Macbeth: Yes I heard an owl and a cricket.

Macbeth:

Lady Macbeth: What a stupid thing to say – a terrible sight indeed!

Macbeth:

Lady Macbeth: Don't think about it so much!

Macbeth:

Lady Macbeth: You can't think like this. We'll go mad!

Macbeth:

Lady Macbeth: Who shouted that? You're being soft, thinking like this. Get some water and wash the blood off your hands. Why did you bring the daggers back? They've got to be by the guards. Go and put them there and rub the blood over the guards.

Macbeth:

Lady Macbeth: You're hopeless. Give me them. Only children are afraid of the dead. If Duncan's body is still bleeding, I'll rub blood over the guards, and they'll look guilty! (*She leaves*)

Macbeth:

Lady Macbeth: (*She comes back*)
Look, my hands are like yours now, but I'm no coward. I can hear knocking. Let's go back to our room. We'll wash there and get rid of the blood. Get your pyjamas on. We can't look as if we know anything. Stop thinking about it!

Macbeth:

Describing the scene of a murder

Macduff finds the body of Duncan. He runs out of the room shouting:

'Awake! awake! Ring the alarum-bell. Murder and treason'

He must have been very shocked to see King Duncan's body.

1 Imagine that you are Macduff. Describe what you saw, when you went into the King's room.

To help you, think about what you know about the murder:

- His guards were lying dead, with blood all over their clothes and faces.
- The daggers were lying by the guards.
- Duncan had been stabbed in his bed. Perhaps he was hanging out of bed.
- There would have been lots of blood.

You might begin your description like this:

I went up to King Duncan's room to wake him up. I thought something was strange because I couldn't hear the guards snoring. I slowly pushed the door open. There, before my eyes, were the bodies of . . .

2 When you have finished, read your description aloud to a partner.
Try to sound shocked and disgusted.
What did your partner think of it?

What does Macduff really think?

Macduff found Duncan's body.
He found it in Macbeth's castle.

1 Read page 23 again, looking at Macduff and what he says.
That is in Shakespeare's language. Now read it again, in
Modern English.

2 Write down what you notice about Macduff.

Ross: Does anyone know who murdered him?
Macduff: *The guards that Macbeth killed.*
Ross: What could they have been thinking of?
Macduff: *They were bribed. Malcolm and Donalbain, King
Duncan's sons, have run away. That makes them
suspects.*
Ross: So – Macbeth will probably become king.
Macduff: *He's already gone to Scone to be crowned.*
Ross: Where's Duncan's body?
Macduff: *In Colme-kill.*
Ross: Are you going to Scone?
Macduff: *No, I'm going to Fife.*
Ross: Well I'm going there.
Macduff: *I hope things go well there. You never know, new
things don't suit everyone!*

Did you notice that Macduff answers with **facts**? He only
gives his **opinion** in the last line.
He must suspect something or somebody, but he never says a
word.

3 Discuss the following with a partner or as a class:

• What do you think he is really thinking, while he is talking
to Ross?
• Why does he decide to go to his home in Fife and not go
to see Macbeth crowned?
• Do you think that he is taking a risk by not going to
Macbeth's coronation?

Writing newspaper headlines

The story of King Duncan's death would be a **SCOOP**.
A **scoop** is a big news story.

Imagine that you are the editor of a newspaper called
Scotland Today. You have to decide on a headline that will
make people buy your newspaper, when they see the front page.

Some of the headlines below have been started, but not
finished.

1 Try to fill in a word or words that will make people stop
and read!

King Found D_____!

Duncan Dead in his B_____

A Shock for the N_____

Malcolm and Donalbain
left without a F_____

Stabbed to D_____

Guards might have m_____ the King

2 Now that you have completed the headlines, try to come
up with two of your own.

3 Once you have done that, draw your headline, thinking
about the font size and the colour.

You might want to put your headline on display with the
others done by your class.

Which headline would persuade you to buy the newspaper?

Drawing your own images

You have now read Act 2.
It is full of **images**.
Images are pictures – not real ones – but pictures that you see in your mind.
They stay with you in your imagination for a long time.
Shakespeare wanted his audience to remember images.

The play is full of horrible events. Shakespeare wanted the audience to be frightened; he used images to make people scared, and also to make them think.
Now that Act 2 has finished, think about the images that you remember from it.

1 Draw some images onto paper, showing the horrible things that went on.
To get you started, think about the answers to these questions.

a What did Macbeth see that he thought showed him the way to Duncan's room?
b What did Lady Macbeth have to ring to give Macbeth the signal that he could go ahead and kill Duncan?
c What did Macbeth have all over his hands after he killed the King?
d What did Lady Macbeth say were the same colour as his, after she had been to return the daggers?
e What did she want to use to clean them up?
f What did Macduff find?
g Did the sun come out the day after the King's death?
h What did Duncan's horses do when Duncan was dead?

Once you have found the answers to these, you will have some images ready to draw.

2 When you have finished your picture, compare it with those done by the rest of the class.

3 Show your work to a teacher who doesn't know what play you are studying. Get the teacher to guess the play – if she/he is right – your picture has worked!

A weather forecast

After the news, a **weather forecaster** usually comes on and tells us what the weather *has been* like and what it *will be* like the next day.
The forecaster uses **stickers** that are put on the map to show the weather.

1 Plan and design the stickers that you would use when describing the weather *before* and *after* Duncan's murder. Remember that people believed that the King was God's representative on Earth. If anything happened to him, there would be trouble on Earth.

On page 22, an old man talks to Ross. His words will help you design stickers.

- 'dark night strangles the travelling lamp.'
- 'A falcon ... was by a mousing owl hawk'd at and kill'd'
- 'And Duncan's horses ... broke their stalls, flung out ... as they would make war ... 'Tis said they ate each other'

Below are two stickers to help you. Draw the others, thinking of what might happen in the future. Think about storms, other animals, the sun and moon.

2 Write the words that go with your stickers and present your forecast to the class.

What has happened so far?

The passage below tells you what has happened in the play so far.
Read it and fill in the blanks so that the sentences make sense. The words in the box below will help you.

Macbeth and Banquo are good _____. After fighting in a battle, they meet three _____, who tell Macbeth that he is going to become Thane of Cawdor and then _____. Macbeth is shocked at this, but excited, because he wants to be king. Banquo doesn't _____ the witches. When Macbeth is told that Duncan has made him _____ of Cawdor, he starts thinking about being king. He sends a letter to his _____, Lady Macbeth, telling her the news. He also tells her that King _____ is going to spend the night at their _____. She persuades Macbeth to kill the King. He isn't too sure, but she talks him into it. He _____ the King and is sorry immediately after. She tells him not to be so stupid. Duncan's _____, Malcolm and Donalbain, run away. That means that Macbeth becomes king.
Not everyone is happy. Macduff isn't! He doesn't go to the _____. Strange things have been happening! Horses have _____ each other; the sun hasn't come out. There is going to be trouble.

Words to help you

Thane   Duncan   murders   friends   eaten   trust
witches   wife   King   castle   sons   coronation

Banquo has his suspicions

Banquo was Macbeth's good friend. Remember that he fought alongside him in the battle.

At the start of Act 3, he is on stage on his own. He is talking to himself. What he says is called a **soliloquy** or a **monologue**.

He says – about Macbeth being king – '**and I fear, Thou play'd most foully for't**'.

Imagine that you are Banquo. You are going to talk about your worries.

Before you can do that, write your worries down. You can then use your piece to perform your **monologue** to the class.

1 To help you write down your worries, consider the following.

What does Banquo already know?

- He knows that the Witches said that Macbeth would be Thane of Cawdor and that came true.
- He knows that the Witches said Macbeth would be king and now he is king.
- He knows that Macbeth rode ahead of King Duncan's party to reach his castle first.
- He knows that Duncan was murdered in Macbeth's castle.
- He knows that Macbeth killed the guards so that it looked like they had killed Duncan.
- He knows that the Witches said that he should be the father of lots of kings.

Can you think of anything else that he knows?

2 When you have thought of everything you need, write your piece.

3 Practise it, before you try to say it aloud to your partner or the class. If you need your written piece, use it, but try not to read it. Try to act as if you are really speaking to yourself.

Hang on a minute!

People say this when they have been thinking about something and they want to tell someone their ideas.
Look at page 25, where Macbeth is alone on stage, worrying about how safe he is as king.

Imagine that you have been listening to Macbeth and you want to tell him what YOU think. You are going to begin your piece with the words: Hang on a minute . . .

But before you can, you have to check what Macbeth is saying.

- 'Our fears in Banquo stick deep'
- 'his royalty of nature'
- 'He hath a wisdom'
- 'They hail'd him father to a line of kings'
- 'they plac'd a fruitless crown and put a barren sceptre in my gripe'
- 'the seeds of Banquo kings!'

He is very upset about Banquo. He is angry that he has killed Duncan to make Banquo's sons kings.

Now, think about what Macbeth already has.

- He is king.
- He has a strong wife.
- He has a castle and servants and comfort.
- He is a brave warrior.
- People will obey him.
- He can order everyone around.
- He will never be hungry.

Perhaps you can think of other things.

You are ready to tell him off! Begin with those words: **Hang on a minute . . .**
Tell him how good his life is and how he should be satisfied now that he has what he wants.

Who is worrying about what?

In this play, people worry about so many things.

Remind yourself of what has happened up until Macbeth tells Lady Macbeth that he has planned something that will happen that night. That is Act 3: Scene 2, pages 27 and 28.

1 Talk with a partner about the things that have taken place.

2 Read the lines below. Each one belongs to a character. See if you can match up the **worry** with the **character**. Draw a line to join the worry to the character.

1. Well, he's King now, just like the Witches promised, but I think that he might have killed Duncan to become King.

2. Whoever killed my father might want to kill me, so I'm off to England.

3. My brother is going to England, and I'm scared, so I'm off to Ireland.

4. What is the matter with him? Why can't he spend more time with me? I'm worried that we can't sleep.

5. I keep having nightmares and I get so mad when I think that I have killed Duncan so that Banquo's sons can be Kings.

6. He's fallen for our predictions. Let's hope that he comes back to us and we can really make him suffer! Our Masters will be happy with us.

7. There's something wrong in Scotland. I think that Macbeth isn't all that he seems. I didn't go to his coronation, so I won't go to his feast.

8. My father seems so worried about something. Maybe he'll talk about what's bothering him while we're out riding.

Helping Fleance escape

1 To help Fleance get past the murderers, you must fill in the blanks in the sentences below. Use pages 24 and 29 to find your answers.

2 You can move from one square to another in any direction, but you mustn't jump back to a square that you have already answered. Each square scores **one** point.

3 Try to get as many points as possible before reaching the end!

- **B**_____ was Fleance's father.
- Banquo called the Witches **W**_____ **W**_____.
- Banquo thought he might be 'the **r**_____ and **f**_____ of many kings.'
- Fleance was staying at **M**_____ castle.
- That night Macbeth said that there was to be a **s**_____ **s**_____.
- Banquo told Macbeth that they were going out **r**_____**g**.
- They were going riding that **a**_____.
- The supper was to start at **s**_____ o'clock.
- A '**f**_____ **c**_____' meant Macbeth had no children.
- A **b**_____ **s**_____' also meant Macbeth had no children.
- There were **th**_____ murderers.
- It was going to **r**_____ that night.
- The murderers heard **h**_____, and that told them that Banquo and Fleance were coming.

A ghost at the table!

On Shakepeare's stage, the actors might have pretended that there was a ghost. It would have been hard to make a ghost appear, even though there was a trap door in the floor of the stage.

Today, it is a lot easier to make ghosts appear, because we have lighting, special effects and the theatre can be completely dark!

It is also a lot easier to make costumes, because we have more materials to use.

1 Imagine that you are the **costume designer**. You have to decide what the **ghost** will look like.

2 Draw a sketch of your ideas, before you present it to the class.

What do you already know about Banquo?

- He was out riding when he was killed. Look at the picture of him on page 29. Perhaps you would like to keep those clothes or perhaps you will have other ideas about his riding gear.
- One murderer said it would rain, so Banquo's body would be wet!
- His throat was cut!
- He had blood in his hair – 'gory locks'
- His head had at least twenty gashes on it – 'twenty mortal murders on their crowns'.

From this, you will have ideas about what he will look like.

3 When you are happy with your sketch, show it to the class. You *must* be able to explain why you have chosen to draw the ghost your way. Use the words of the play to help you.

Designing the stage set

Imagine that you are the person who has to design the **set** for the banquet scene. This will be an important scene because the ghost of Banquo has to appear and frighten Macbeth.

1 Read pages 30, 31, 32, and 33 again to get an idea of:

- what props or furniture must be on stage
- where the actors must be sat for the audience to see them
- where Macbeth and Lady Macbeth can go to talk quietly when she tells him to stop being so stupid and go back to the table
- how the ghost can come onto the stage and sit at the table.

What kind of **table** will you have? Remember there will be lots of thanes there. What kind of **chairs** will you have? Will Macbeth have a special chair, because he is king?
What will you have on the table? Plates? Glasses? Knives? Forks? Food?
Where will the **door** be? Macbeth has to go to it to talk to the murderer. The thanes have to leave by the door.
Will you have a **pillar** or a **window** where Lady Macbeth can talk to Macbeth quietly? How will the ghost come in? Will he sit at Macbeth's chair?

2 When you have answered these questions and worked out your ideas, draw your set.

3 Show your sketch to a partner to share your ideas. When you talk about your ideas you must be able to explain why you have made certain decisions.

4 Make a model of your **stage set**, by using cardboard boxes, card, materials, so that you can present it in a 3D way. Your Technology teacher might be able to help out with materials and tools.
If you do this, take a photograph of your work, so that you can save the **evidence.**
You won't be able to store your stage set for that long.

Dramatising a scene

Read pages 31 and 32 again.
This is the scene where Macbeth is giving a feast for his noblemen. His wife is also there. Banquo has been murdered, and his ghost comes to the table and sits on a chair. This terrifies Macbeth. Only he can see the ghost. Lady Macbeth has to cover up for him. Eventually, the noblemen leave because Macbeth is acting so strangely.

Read the **text** (words said) again.
In a group of FIVE, you can dramatise the scene.

1 Read your parts first, trying to put feeling into the words. If you prefer to use Modern English, 'translate' the **text**, so that it still makes sense.

- Whoever plays Banquo will have nothing to say, but that person must think about how to move and what to do with her/his arms and face.
- Perhaps Banquo will point at Macbeth.
- Perhaps Banquo will smile horribly and move around Macbeth, pulling faces.
- He will definitely 'shake his gory locks' at Macbeth.
- He will 'nod' his head as well.
- The words will sometimes tell you what to do, especially when Banquo has to appear and disappear.

2 When you think you have the main points ready to act out, find a space to do it. Remember that movement and body language will be really important.

- Ross and Lenox will not know what's going on.
- Lady Macbeth will not know what's going on, but she will be cross with Macbeth.
- Only Macbeth can see Banquo.
- To try to calm Macbeth down, Lady Macbeth makes everyone lift their glasses to drink to their king – on the line 'Come, love and health to all ...'
- Ross and Lenox will leave in a very puzzled mood.

What do you think of that?

People often say those words when something has shocked or surprised them?
Can you think of any times when you have heard those words said?
If so, share them with the group.
After the banquet scene, Ross and Lenox will be surprised and shocked. They have just seen their king behaving very strangely indeed.

With a partner, write the **script** of the conversation Ross and Lenox have as they ride away from Macbeth's castle together. You might want to act it out.

Remember what they have seen:

- the table set with lots of food and drink
- Lady Macbeth dressed up for a feast
- Macbeth ready to eat and drink.

Then:

- Macbeth going to the door and talking quietly
- Macbeth coming back to the table but not sitting down
- Macbeth shouting at an empty chair
- Lady Macbeth making excuses and talking to Macbeth in whispers
- Macbeth getting back to normal and then shouting again
- Lady Macbeth telling them to leave.

Of course, in your script, you must talk about *what* Macbeth said, because those words are very interesting!
You will be suspicious now. Perhaps you will be worried about your own safety.
You will probably be wondering why Banquo didn't turn up. After all, he was going to come. You will also be wondering why Macduff didn't come and where they both have got to.

A spy's report – in code!

Did you notice that, on page 33, Macbeth told Lady Macbeth that:

'There's not a one of them, but in his house I keep a servant fee'd'?

This means that Macbeth has a spy in every nobleman's house. Do you think he trusts people?

He is angry that Macduff did not turn up to his banquet. He heard from somebody – probably a spy – that Macduff wasn't going to turn up.

If you were a spy, you wouldn't want to write messages so that anybody could read them. You would probably use a **code**.

1 Try to crack this code and find out what the message says! The answers to the problems equal letters.

A	B	C	D	E	F	G	H	I	J	K	L	M
1	2	3	4	5	6	7	8	9	10	11	12	13

N	O	P	Q	R	S	T	U	V	W	X	Y	Z
14	15	16	17	18	19	20	21	22	23	24	25	26

$12 + 1 = \square$ $2 - 1 = \square$ $2 + 1 = \square$ $2 \times 2 = \square$
$7 \times 3 = \square$ $2 \times 3 = \square$ $5 + 1 = \square$ $4 \times 2 = \square$
$1 \times 1 = \square$ $18 + 1 = \square$ $8 - 1 = \square$ $3 \times 5 = \square$
$2 \times 7 = \square$ $4 + 1 = \square$ $10 \times 2 = \square$ $14 + 1 = \square$
$6 - 1 = \square$ $20 - 6 = \square$ $10 - 3 = \square$ $3 \times 4 = \square$
$15 - 14 = \square$ $8 + 6 = \square$ $9 - 5 = \square$

$4 \times 3 = \square$ $10 - 5 = \square$ $13 - 7 = \square$ $10 \times 2 = \square$
$9 - 1 = \square$ $3 \times 3 = \square$ $20 - 1 = \square$ $21 + 2 = \square$
$5 + 4 = \square$ $5 + 1 = \square$ $8 - 3 = \square$ $7 - 6 = \square$
$6 \times 2 = \square$ $10 + 5 = \square$ $12 + 2 = \square$ $19 - 14 = \square$

2 Now see if you can write your own message, either using this code or making up one of your own, for your partner to work out.

Different points of view

Let's look at things that have happened in the play from THREE different points of view:

● the audience's   ● Macbeth's   ● Ross's

Below are sentences that tell you what has happened in the play so far.

1 In the three columns opposite, tick if they know what has happened; cross if they don't.
The first one has been done for you.

	Macbeth	Ross	Audience
I The Witches told Macbeth he would be king.	√	×	√
2 Macbeth killed King Duncan.			
3 Banquo said the Witches might be evil.			
4 Malcolm has gone to England.			
5 Macduff suspects Macbeth.			
6 Banquo suspects Macbeth.			
7 Lady Macbeth is having nightmares.			
8 Banquo is murdered.			
9 Fleance has escaped.			
10 Macbeth plotted Banquo's murder.			
12 A ghost appeared at the banquet.			
13 The ghost was Banquo's.			
14 Macbeth has spies in every castle.			

2 From this chart, you can see that Ross, who is a Scottish nobleman, doesn't know much.
What does that tell you about the state of Scotland under Macbeth's rule?

3 It is important that the audience knows more than the characters. Why?

4 At the end of Act 3, who do you most feel sorry for?

A recipe for disaster!

Remember when Macbeth goes to see the Witches (pages 36 to 38) and demands that their masters show him what the future holds?

The Witches cooked up a **recipe for disaster** for Macbeth when they threw the ingredients into their cauldron and made predictions that fooled him!

Lets look at the things they throw into their cauldron:

Toad, that under cold stone	
Days and nights has thirty-one	
Swelter'd venom, sleeping got,	sweaty poison
Boil thou first i'th' charmed pot ...	
Fillet of a fenny snake,	
In the cauldron boil and bake,	
Eye of newt, and toe of frog,	
Wool of bat, and tongue of dog,	
Adder's fork, and blind-worm's sting,	forked tongue
Lizard's leg, and howlet's wing ...	
Scale of dragon, tooth of wolf ...	
Gall of goat, and slip of **yew**	a tree thought to be poisonous
Sliver'd in the **moon's eclipse** ...	cut off an unlucky time
Cool it with a baboon's blood ...	
Double, double toil and trouble;	
Fire burn, and cauldron bubble.	

What a **revolting recipe**! Even the Witches say it's like a **hell-broth**!

1 List the ingredients for another revolting recipe! This time YOURS!

If you can, make every two lines rhyme!

2 Now read it out loud.
You can measure how revolting it was by the number of **yuks!** you got from your class!

In the kitchen of the Three Witches!

Read pages 36 to 38 again.

This is a very important scene, because THIS time, instead of the Witches meeting Macbeth, HE goes to search them out. It could be a very scary scene on stage.

1 Describe what the stage would look like.
You need to think of:

- where they would be – in a cave, on the heath?
- what the cauldron would look like
- would there be any smoke?
- where the Witches would get their ingredients from?
- would there be explosions when the spirits appear?
- whether the Witches would laugh/cackle when Macbeth calls them **'black and midnight hags'** and then later, **'Filthy hags'**
- how the Witches would disappear
- what Macbeth would be doing all through the scene
- what kind of lighting there would be on your stage.

2 Share your ideas with your partner and present them to the class.

He feels safe, but he's being tricked!

The Witches have called their masters, and the Spirits have told Macbeth that he must be brave and, **'laugh to scorn the power of man, for none of woman born shall harm Macbeth.'**
He doesn't care about Macduff now. Remember that Macduff didn't turn up to Macbeth's banquet!
The Spirits then tell him he will never be conquered, **'until great Birnam Wood to high Dunsinane hill shall come against him.'**
He doesn't feels scared now, because no forest can walk up a hill.

Look at page 38.
Nothing that the Spirits have said has worried Macbeth so far ...
What is he shown that really bothers him now?
If you had to illustrate the nightmares that Macbeth is having, you now have a very good idea of the things that he would dream of.

1 On a very large piece of paper, either draw the pictures you think would haunt Macbeth or collect pictures from magazines and cut them out to paste them on paper to explain what haunts Macbeth.

2 Present your **nightmare picture** to the class.
You must be able to explain why you have chosen to use certain pictures. You can go back to the words of the text to help you.

Writing a newspaper report

When Macbeth finds out that Macduff has gone to England, he is angry.
Look at page 38.
He says he will, **'give to th' edge o' th' sword his wife, his babes and all unfortunate souls that trace him in his line.'**
He is determined to have every person in Macduff's family killed.

Read page 39 again.
Two people try to warn Lady Macduff about what might happen, but she is murdered.
You are going to write the newspaper report that will follow her murder.

1 Remember that a newspaper report must tell the reader:

- **what** happened
- **where** it happened
- **when** it happened
- **who** might have done the deed
- **why** they might have done it.

You know **what** happened – Lady Macduff was killed. You know **where** it happened – in the castle at Fife. You will have to make up the other details from what you know of the play.

2 Remember to make up a headline that is eye-catching. It must mention the **brutal murder** of the Macduffs.

3 Remember to write it in columns.

4 If you can, type up your report on the computer so that it looks more like a real report.

The Doctor's notes I

Read Act 5: Scene 1 again on pages 43 and 44.

The Gentlewoman, Lady Macbeth's servant, tells the doctor that Lady Macbeth has been sleepwalking.
Have you ever done this? Ask your parents! If you have, what did you say and do?

Lady Macbeth has a **guilty conscience**. She doesn't sleep well. She is having nightmares.
The doctor says, **'I will set down what comes from her'**. This means that he will make notes.

Imagine that you are the doctor. Write down what Lady Macbeth does and says.

(Continued on Sheet 2)

The Doctor's notes 2

(Continued from Sheet 1)

Answer these questions to help you.

- Does she have a light (a candle) with her?
- Are her eyes open or closed?
- What does she do with her hands – for over a quarter of an hour at times
- What does she see on her hands?
- **''tis time to do't'** – time to do what?
- **'A soldier and afeared?'** Who is she talking to?
- **'who would have thought the old man to have so much blood'** Who is this?
- **'The Thane of Fife had a wife'** Who is she talking about?
- **'Banquo's buried'** Macbeth must have told her what he had done to Banquo.
- **'there's knocking at the gate'** When did they hear this?

The doctor would note down all of this and perhaps he would guess at what she is talking about. After all, he does say **'foul whisperings are abroad'** which means that he must have heard rumours about Macbeth and his wife.

You might begin your notes like this:

On the night of 2 July I went to the Queen's bedroom.
Her servant had asked me to watch the Queen. She
got up out of bed, held a candle in her hand and ...

Look into my eyes. You are feeling sleepy

Have you ever heard those words said?
Probably when you have been watching someone **hypnotise** someone else. There have been lots of television programmes where this has happened. People go back to 'other lives' and even act like animals.

1 Imagine that the doctor could have **hypnotised** Lady Macbeth.
Look at the questions he might have asked her, and try to give her answers.
Remember she wouldn't lie under hypnosis.

Why do you keep rubbing your hands?	
What spot are you talking about?	
Who is the soldier who is frightened?	
Who is the old man you're talking about?	
What do you know about the Thane of Fife?	
Where do you think his wife is now?	
Tell me all you know about Banquo!	
Why can't you sleep well?	

2 When you have answered the questions, you can work with a partner and act out one of your **hypnosis scenes** to the class. Listen to what they say so that you can improve your work.

Two costumes for Lady Macbeth

It is really important that the audience see a change in Lady Macbeth.

At the start – she is strong and determined to have Macbeth king and herself, queen. She plans Duncan's murder. She persuades Macbeth to do the killing. She tells him not to worry about the murder. She covers up for him at the banquet.

At the end – she is feeling guilty. She can't sleep. She doesn't see much of her husband. She can't cope with her thoughts. She is going mad! She takes her own life.

What she wears will tell the audience what she is like.

1 You must decide what she will wear:
– during the banquet scene
– during the sleepwalking scene.

What effect do you want? To help you decide, think about these points:

In the banquet scene, she is powerful; she is queen; she thinks fast; she covers up for her husband.

- What colour dress will she wear?
- What will her hair be like?
- What shoes will she have on?
- Will she wear any jewellery?

In the sleepwalking scene, she is weak; she is still queen; she thinks about the past and what she has done; she thinks about her husband.

- What will she wear?
- What will her hair be like?
- Will she be wearing any shoes?

2 When you have drawn your designs, present them to the class. You must be able to give very good reasons why you have chosen the costumes. For example – if you have chosen a red dress for the banquet, that might be because she is linked with blood. Be ready to explain your reasons.

The battle for Scotland

In Act 5, the last Act of the play, the battle for Scotland has lots of action in it. The scenes are very fast and they change quickly from one side to the other.

Below are sentences that plot the progress of the battle. They begin at Act 5: Scene 2 (page 45).

1 They are not in the correct order. What you must do is put them in the right order so that they make sense. Use the play to make sure that you are following the action.

a A messenger tells Macbeth that Birnam Wood is moving.

b Malcolm leads the English soldiers against Scotland and the nobles discuss their plans.

c Macbeth's messenger says that he has seen 10,000 soldiers.

d Macbeth is told that Lady Macbeth is dead.

e Only soldiers who are forced to serve Macbeth are staying – the rest are deserting.

f Macbeth has put troops around Dunsinane, but most of his soldiers do not want to serve him.

g Macduff finds Macbeth and they fight until Macbeth is killed.

h Malcolm is King of Scotland.

i Macbeth asks Seyton to help him put on his armour.

j Young Siward and Macbeth fight and the young boy is killed.

k Macbeth talks to the doctor about Lady Macbeth.

l Malcolm tells his troops to cut down branches from Birnam Wood and carry them in front of their bodies to hide their numbers.

2 Once you have done that, check your answers with a partner to see whether you both agree on the way that the action develops on stage.

Same line – different meaning

On page 49, Macbeth is told that his wife is dead, and he says: **'She should have died hereafter.'**

People who discuss Shakespeare's plays have thought about what Macbeth meant and suggested these ideas:

- She would died sometime anyway.
- She should have died at a more convenient time.
- She should have died when I could have mourned her properly.
- Now's not the time for her to die, because all I remember are awful times.

Did Macbeth love her? Which of these things do you think he might have meant?

1 To help you decide, think back over the play. What do the following statements prove? Write your answers in the boxes.

Statement	What does it prove?
Macbeth sent his wife a letter telling her what the Witches had promised.	
Lady Macbeth wanted Macbeth to be king.	
She persuaded him to kill Duncan.	
She insulted him and made him feel guilty.	
She planned the murder.	
She took the daggers back when Macbeth messed things up.	
She fainted – or pretended to – when Macbeth was about to give himself away.	
She covered up for him at the banquet.	
He spent time away from her.	
He didn't tell her about his plans for Banquo.	

Did they love each other? Did that love last until the end?

2 When you have decided, share your ideas with a partner.

Doing two things at the same time

Imagine how hard it must have been for Macbeth and Macduff to **fight and talk** at the same time.
Look at pages 53 and 54.
This is where they meet on the battlefield. They fight, but look at how much they say to each other while they are fighting.

To see how this is done on stage, work with a partner to **dramatise** the scene. You will have to act this out *and* talk at the same time. You might work out where you can stop to speak.

Would you, for example:

- stand and study your enemy?
- fight and then jump on something high, like a rock, and speak, before you carried on?

There are lots of ways you can act it out. Acting it out helps you realise how the action on stage takes place. It can be fun.

But – be careful and be sensible: professional stage fighters **never** hurt each other. Because you are not a professional, you must follow rules when you stage fight – don't touch each other; don't use any props that will hurt; pretend rather than hold any object; move around your enemy; if you fall, fall slowly.

The one that got away

Below are nine sentences.
The start of each sentence does not fit the end. They have been mixed up.

1 Match up the beginning of every sentence with the correct ending, so that they tell you what happened to the characters. And find – the one that got away!

a Banquo was ... killed but escaped in the dark!
b Macbeth was ... murdered while out riding at night.
c Duncan was ... executed for treason.
d The grooms were ... killed while fighting with Macbeth.
e Lady Macbeth was ... murdered in her castle with her children.
f The first Thane of Cawdor was ... murdered by Macbeth.
g Lady Macduff was ... killed and his head chopped off.
h Young Siward was ... stabbed while drunk.
i Fleance wasn't ... a victim of suicide.

2 Who was the lucky one?
Think about him and the other characters.
How many of them do you feel sorry for?

3 Talk about this with a partner. Make notes about your choices, so that your reasons are clear. When you finish, report your decisions to the rest of the class.
Did the class come up with the same characters and the same reasons?

True or false?

The sentences below give you facts about the play *Macbeth*
. . . or do they?
Some of the statements are **true**; some are **false**.
It's up to you to decide! Put T or F in the boxes.

1 There are three witches. ☐
2 The name of the traitor, whom King Duncan had put to death, was Coward. ☐
3 When they first met Macbeth and Banquo, the Witches would not speak to Banquo until they had spoken to Macbeth first. ☐
4 King Duncan's sons are Malcolm and Donalbain. ☐
5 Lady Macbeth has to persuade Macbeth to kill the King, because he has second thoughts about it. ☐
6 The plan to kill Duncan was that Lady Macbeth would stab the guards and then Macbeth would kill the King. ☐
7 Macbeth messed up the plan by bringing the daggers back with him. ☐
8 Malcolm escaped to England and Donalbain to France. ☐
9 Macbeth arranges Banquo's murder without telling his wife of his plan. ☐
10 Fleance, Banquo's son, kills one of the murderers before he runs away. ☐
11 Banquo's ghost sits down on a chair at the banquet. ☐
12 Macbeth keeps spies in as many noblemen's houses as he can. ☐
13 The Witches call their masters when Macbeth goes to them for more predictions. ☐
14 They tell him that he is safe until the Scottish hills move towards his castle. ☐
15 Macduff goes to England to get help off Malcolm. ☐
16 Malcolm puts Macduff to the test to make sure that he is telling the truth. ☐
17 Lady Macbeth tells the doctor about the crimes she has done and he gives her poison to kill herself with. ☐
18 Macbeth learns that Macduff was born of woman. ☐
19 Macbeth is killed by Macduff. ☐
20 Malcolm becomes the Prince of Scotland. ☐

When you find the false sentences – correct them so that they are true!

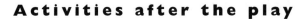
A word of warning ... beware ...

Macbeth thinks that the Witches can predict the future. He believes what they tell him, and when he knows they have tricked him it is too late!
Imagine that other predictions are made. This time they tell the truth.

1 Read the words below and decide which characters the predictions were made for.
Write in their names.

1. You will be great, and get what you want. Be careful, because what you want will not last. You will end up scared and sad. You will become ill and do something very foolish!

2. You will always be a good person. Other people you think are good friends turn out to be evil. Be careful when you answer questions. Your answers will be used against you! Take care if you go riding at night!

3. You will be frightened at first. You will try to escape to another country. But, you will have to return and save your people. Take care and trust no-one until you are sure they are your friends!

4. There will be very sad times ahead, when your family will suffer. You will also suffer, because you will try to save your country. Be careful when you fight against a brave warrior!

5. You might get what you want by playing with other people's feelings, but there are beings higher than you – your masters! And if they are not happy – beware!

Have you worked out who they are?

2 When you have done that, choose one character of your own and try to predict the future for them, using the play to help you. You might choose Duncan, Donalbain or Lady Macduff.

What kind of a person are you? I

Imagine that the following quiz appears in a magazine read by Lady Macbeth.

Try to answer the questions **as if you are Lady Macbeth**.
How would you answer?
Circle either: **a**, **b**, or **c**.
Check your answers at the end.

1 You are told that one day you will rule your country with your partner. Do you:
   a. say, 'Don't be daft!'
   b. say, 'OK, I'll wait and see. It might happen!'
   c. do anything to make it happen.

2 Your partner refuses to do something really important. Even though you know it's wrong, do you:
   a. go on and on to him, until he agrees to do it
   b. say, 'Fine, we won't bother!'
   c. call him a coward, walk off and forget about it.

3 Your partner messes up a very important plan. Would you say:
   a. 'Don't worry, it doesn't matter.'
   b. 'You idiot! I'll finish it off!'
   c. 'You've done well so far.'

4 You have both done something really bad. Your partner is about to give the game away. Do you:
   a. run off and let him suffer
   b. faint to take the pressure off him
   c. push him into another room and tell him to shut up.

5 Your partner is worried about a crime he has committed. Do you:
   a. tell him to confess
   b. leave him
   c. tell him not to worry too much about it.

(Continued on Sheet 2)

What kind of person are you? 2

(Continued from Sheet 1)

6 Your partner is planning something. He won't tell you what it is. Do you:
  a. wait for the surprise
  b. nag him until he tells you
  c. forget about it.

7 He shows you up at a meal with friends. Do you:
  a. leave and go to bed
  b. carry on as if nothing is wrong
  c. lie and tell his friends to go because he is ill.

8 He is spending a lot of time alone. Do you:
  a. think 'Good. I'm fed up of him!'
  b. ask him what's wrong because you're worried
  c. go and stay with a friend until he sorts himself out.

9 He tells you he is going to visit some women who have been advising him. Do you:
  a. not really care because you're tired and not sure what is going on
  b. follow him
  c. say that you're going too.

10 Your relationship has broken up. You're so fed up. You can't sleep at night. Do you:
  a. go to the doctor
  b. talk to your husband about it
  c. do nothing though you know you're not well.

How did you do?

Answers: 1c, 2a, 3b, 4b, 5c, 6a, 7c, 8b, 9a, 10c

If you got most right: Well done.
If you got most answers wrong: You need to go over Lady Macbeth's character again to learn more about her.

You lied to me! I

These might be the words that Macbeth would say to the Witches if he had the chance to speak to them just before being killed by Macduff.

1 On Sheet 2 is a script. It has Macbeth's words but not the Witches' words. Those words are at the end of the script. Put their words in the right places, so that the script makes sense.

2 When you have completed the script so that it makes sense, read it with a partner. Try to think of how your voice will sound and how fast or slow you will speak.

3 Once you have done this, talk with your partner about the Witches.

- Do you think that they *made* Macbeth do anything?
- Do you think that Macbeth was to blame for everything that he did?
- Do you think that Lady Macbeth was mostly to blame?

On trial

4 Choose people in the class to take the parts of Macbeth, Lady Macbeth, the Third Witch, and any other person you think should go to Macbeth's trial.

a You will need time to think up questions to ask. The people taking roles will also have to think about how they will answer questions.

b Now put the characters on trial, by **hot-seating** them. This means that you question the character and she/he answers as if she/he is that character.

c When all the questions have been asked and all the answers given, take a vote.

Who was most to blame for all that happened?
Macbeth? Lady Macbeth? The Three Witches?

(Continued on Sheet 2)

You lied to me! 2

(Continued from Sheet 1)

Macbeth: You lied to me when we first met!

Witches:

Macbeth: Yes, but you told me I'd be king. You didn't tell me that I had to kill to become king.

Witches:

Macbeth: You didn't tell me that I'd suffer and I wouldn't be able to sleep!

Witches:

Macbeth: Yes you did tell me about Banquo, but that made me so angry that I had to have him killed too. Why didn't you warn me that I'd have to kill him, if I became king?

Witches:

Macbeth: I chose to visit you and you told me a pack of lies.

Witches:

Macbeth: You didn't tell me that the soldiers would cut down branches and that way Birnam Wood would move!

Witches:

Macbeth: You never told me Macduff was ripped from his mother's womb

Witches:

- You didn't ask. Everything you did was your fault. Now go. Leave us alone.

- No, when we first met, we said you'd be Thane of Cawdor and you were!

- You suffered because you felt guilty. Anyway, we told you about Banquo!

- When you visited us, we told you the truth. You didn't listen.

- Nobody told you to kill to become king. You decided that.

- You should have thought about how trees can be cut down.

- You chose to have Banquo killed, like you chose to do everything else.

Word games

Can you add a letter and rearrange the word to come up with another?
The first one is done for you.

● Can you add a letter P to **delay** to explain what the Witches did with Macbeth's feelings?

The answer is **played**, because the witches **played** with Macbeth's feelings to make him think he could succeed in his plans.

Now try the following. You can write in your answers.

1 Can you add the letter B to *vera* to make a word that describes Macbeth in battle? _____

2 Can you add the letter R to *shoe* to make the animal that Macbeth rode on in battle? _____

3 Can you add the letter V to *near* to name the bird that Lady Macbeth describes before Duncan comes to her home? _____

4 Can you add the letter C to *least* to find the building in which Duncan was murdered? _____

5 Can you add the letter G to *grade* to find the weapon that Macbeth thinks he sees showing him the way to Duncan's room? _____

6 Can you add the letter O to *ally* to describe what Banquo is like to Macbeth, even though he is suspicious? _____

7 Can you add the letter S to *peel* to explain what Macbeth and Lady Macbeth can't do, because they feel guilty? _____

8 Can you add the letter G to *shot* to explain what sat on Macbeth's chair in the banquet scene and made him scared? _____

9 Can you add the letter R to *may* to describe what Malcolm and Macduff led from England to Scotland to fight with Macbeth? _____

10 Can you add the letter T to *cherub* to find the word that Malcolm uses to describe Macbeth at the end of the play? _____

Solve the clues

These seven clues lead to seven words, whose first letters spell out the name of something or someone in *Macbeth*.

1 The crime that Macbeth committed to become king.

2 Lady Macbeth says of Macbeth: 'Thou wouldst be great. Art not without _____'

3 The Thane of _____ was a traitor and was executed.

4 The name of the king whom Macbeth killed.

5 The Old Man, talking to Ross, says about the night and the killing: ''Tis _____'

6 Complete the line: 'Fair is _____ and foul is fair.'

7 The name of Banquo's son.

These five clues lead to five words, whose first letters spell out the name of something or someone in *Macbeth*.

1 The Third Witch knew when the battle would end. She said: 'That will be ere the set of _____'.

2 Macbeth had none of these but Macduff did, and Macbeth had them killed.

3 The bird of the night that Lady Macbeth heard.

4 Nearly all the scenes in the play take place at _____.

5 The name of the country where Malcolm went after his father's death.

These six clues lead to six words, whose first letters spell out the name of someone or something in *Macbeth*.

1 The cat the First Witch speaks to in the opening scene.

2 Complete the lines: 'When shall we three meet again. In thunder, _____ or in rain.'

3 The word that Macbeth could not say after he had murdered Duncan.

4 The name of the Prince of Cumberland, Duncan's son.

5 The name of the country where Donalbain went after his father's death.

6 What Lady Macbeth was doing while the Doctor watched her. She was _____.

Designing a backcloth

Do you remember, even before you read the play, you looked at the book cover and the **symbols**? You tried to work out what they told you about the play?
You also worked on the Elizabethan theatre. Do you remember that they had very little scenery?

Look again at the photograph of the Globe's stage (page 4 of the *Teacher's Resource Book*). Can you see the doors at the back? Can you see those curtains at the side of the doors?
If the play was going to be a comedy, those curtains or hangings would have bright colours. If the play was going to be a tragedy, those hangings would have dark colours.

Imagine that you have been given the job of designing the hangings for the background to *Macbeth*.
What would you want them to look like?

1 Here are some ideas to help you:

- What things, like humans, fooled Macbeth?
- What did Macbeth think would turn the sea from green to red, if he washed them in it?
- What did Malcolm bring on stage at the end to prove that he had killed Macbeth?

Do you think you could use any of these **symbols** on your backcloth?

2 What about colours?

- At what time of the day did most of the play take place?
- What did Lady Macbeth want to wash off her hands when she was sleepwalking?
- What colour is a raven?

Do you think you could use these **colours** to help you make a spooky backcloth?

Surprise! Surprise!

There are so many shocks and surprises in the play *Macbeth* – not one of them is very pleasant!

Work out the order in which these surprises come in the play.

1 Macbeth is shocked when he finds out that Macduff is not born of woman.
2 Macbeth is surprised when the Witches meet him and Banquo and make predictions.
3 The Doctor is shocked at Lady Macbeth's words when she is sleepwalking.
4 Duncan is surprised that Macbeth has arrived at the castle before him.
5 The thanes are surprised at Macbeth's behaviour during the banquet.
6 Everyone, except Macbeth and his wife are shocked at Duncan's death.
7 Lady Macduff is surprised that Macduff has gone to England, leaving his family.
8 Macbeth is shocked to see Birnam Wood moving.
9 Macduff is surprised at Malcolm's behaviour in England.
10 Macbeth is shocked when he is made Thane of Cawdor, just after the predictions.
11 Macbeth is surprised that Duncan says Malcolm will be the next king.
12 Banquo is surprised when the murderers jump out at him.
13 Lady Macbeth is surprised at Macbeth's letter, telling her about the Witches.

You can write the correct order here: _____

A game of chance

This is what Macbeth played when he first decided to kill Duncan. He took chances. He was never sure of what would happen. He didn't always feel safe.

Try to make your own game of chance.
You have probably made this game before.

1 Take a **square** piece of paper.
2 Fold it in half, making a crease down the half-way mark.
3 Open it up and fold it in half the other way, making a crease.
4 Open it up. Where the crease marks cross is the middle.
5 Fold each corner into the middle point.
6 Turn it over and fold those corners into the middle point.
7 Fold it in half. You will now have four pockets in which to put your fingers.
8 On these four, write the names of characters from the play.
9 On the inside eight triangles, write the names of animals or weapons that are in the play.
10 Underneath each triangle, write something silly that your partner has to do, for example:
'Turn round three times and touch the floor.'
or
'Write your name with your eyes closed.'

Play the game of chance with your partner by moving your fingers in the pockets the number of times the word chosen has letters. On the third go, open the triangle – it's your partner's turn to do the silly thing!

Can you see how stupid Macbeth was to play a game of chance? He never knew what would happen.

And they all lived happily ever after

Not in this play!

Fairy stories usually end with the phrase: **'and they all lived happily ever after'**.

The play *Macbeth* isn't a fairy story but it could still be a very good story to tell younger children.

1 Think about all the **ingredients** that are in the play. The word **ingredients** means what the play is made up of. Make a list of some of these. For example:

- goodies and baddies – with the goodies winning at the end
- violence and murders
- evil witches
- a ghost
- scary moments, like the fighting, the murders and the banquet scene
- a mean, frightening man with an evil wife.

Think about some of the fairy stories you were told when you were younger. They had some of these ingredients.

2 Write the story of *Macbeth* for children who are aged about eight. You can put pictures in your story.

You might want to begin your story like this:

> Once upon a time, there lived a man who was a very brave warrior. He had a wife, but sadly no children. They lived in a big castle ...

When you have finished drafting your story, you could type it out so that it looks more like a real book.

3 Your teacher might arrange a trip to your local Primary school where you can read your story to a small group of eight year olds. You will be able to ask them what they think of it – that will help you to **evaluate** your work.